D0468403

MATHWORKS!

Using Math in the ER

by Hilary Koll, Steve Mills,
and Dr. Kerrie Whitwell

Math and Curriculum Consultant:
Debra Voege, Science and Math
Curriculum Resource Teacher

GARETH**STEVENS**
GS
PUBLISHING
A Member of the WRC Media Family of Companies

Please visit our web site at: **www.garethstevens.com**
For a free color catalog describing Gareth Stevens Publishing's
list of high-quality books and multimedia programs, call
1-800-542-2595 (USA) or 1-800-387-3178 (Canada).
Gareth Stevens Publishing's fax: (414) 332-3567.

Library of Congress Cataloging-in-Publication Data

Koll, Hilary.
    Using math in the ER / Hilary Koll, Steve Mills, and
Kerrie Whitwell. — North American ed.
        p. cm. — (Mathworks!)
    ISBN-10: 0-8368-6762-9 — ISBN-13: 978-0-8368-6762-6 (lib. bdg.)
    ISBN-10: 0-8368-6769-6 — ISBN-13: 978-0-8368-6769-5 (softcover)
    1. Mathematics—Problems, exercises, etc.—Juvenile literature.
2. Hospitals—Emergency service—Juvenile literature. I. Mills,
Steve, 1955- II. Whitwell, Kerrie. III. Title. IV. Series.
QA43.K62   2006
510.76—dc22   2006044345

This North American edition first published in 2007 by
Gareth Stevens Publishing
A Member of the WRC Media Family of Companies
330 West Olive Street, Suite 100
Milwaukee, Wisconsin 53212

This U.S. edition copyright © 2007 by Gareth Stevens, Inc.
Original edition copyright © 2006 by ticktock Entertainment
Ltd. First published in Great Britain in 2006 by ticktock Media
Ltd., Unit 2, Orchard Business Centre, North Farm Road,
Tunbridge Wells, Kent, TN2 3XF, United Kingdom.

Medical Consultant: Dr. Kerrie Whitwell has specialized in
emergency medicine since 1998. Her work includes review
clinics and supervising an observation ward, along with patient
assessment and treatment in an emergency department that
sees more than seventy thousand patients a year.

Gareth Stevens Editor: Dorothy L. Gibbs
Gareth Stevens Art Direction: Tammy West

Photo credits (t=top, b=bottom, c=center, l=left, r=right)
Creatas: 1, 14-15, 22-23, 26-27. Shutterstock: 6-7 (Michael
Ledray), 20-21 (Jaimie Duplass), 24br (Jack Dagley Photography).
StockDisc: 8-9, 10-11, 12-13, 18-19, 24-25, 29br. Science Photo
Library: 16-17 (Ian Hooton).

Every effort has been made to trace the copyright holders
for the photos used in this book. The publisher apologizes,
in advance, for any unintentional omissions and would be
pleased to insert the appropriate acknowledgements in
any subsequent edition of this publication.

All rights reserved to Gareth Stevens, Inc. No part of
this book may be reproduced, stored in a retrieval system,
or transmitted in any form or by any means, electronic,
mechanical, photocopying, recording, or otherwise, without
the prior written permission of the publisher.

Printed in the United States of America

1 2 3 4 5 6 7 8 9 10 09 08 07 06

CONTENTS

Property of Dexter
Middle School Library

HAVE FUN WITH MATH

How to Use This Book

Math is important in the lives of people everywhere. We use math when we play games, ride bicycles, or go shopping, and everyone uses math at work. Imagine you are a nurse or a doctor in a busy hospital emergency room. You may not realize it, but doctors and nurses use math in some way almost every time they treat an illness or an injury. In this book, you will be able to try lots of exciting math activities, using real-life data and facts about hospitals and medicine. If you can work with numbers, measurements, shapes, charts, and diagrams, then you could WORK IN AN ER.

How does it feel to save a life?

Grab your stethoscope and find out what it is like to treat life-threatening illnesses and injuries.

Math Activities

The emergency clipboards have math activities for you to try. Get your pencil, ruler, and notebook (for figuring out problems and listing answers).

BODY TEMPERATURE

Another job for an ER nurse is taking a patient's temperature. A body temperature that is too high or too low can be very serious. When body temperature is high, the patient has a fever and feels warm or hot to the touch. Body temperature that is too low can affect the brain, making the person unable to think clearly or move normally. When a patient's temperature is not normal, a doctor or a nurse will take steps to correct it. In the case of a fever, a nurse might use a damp cloth, or even ice packs, to cool the patient. For a low temperature, or hypothermia, the nurse might cover the patient with a warm-air blanket.

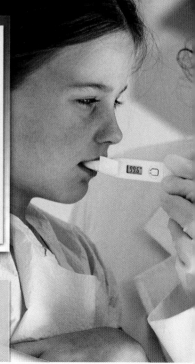

Emergency Work

The DATA BOX on page 15 contains a graph that records a patient's body temperature for one day. Use the graph to help you answer these questions.

1) What was the patient's temperature at
   a) 8:10?
   b) 10:45?
   c) 9:10?

2) At what time was the temperature the lowest?

3) At what time was the temperature 101.3 °F?

4) How many minutes after the first time the temperature was taken was it taken again?

First Aid Tips
• When you are stuck in very cold conditions, do not jump around. The exercise will make you lose heat more quickly.
• About 30 percent of body heat is lost from the head, so make sure you head is covered.

14

NEED HELP?

- If you are not sure how to do some of the math problems, turn to pages 28 and 29, where you will find lots of tips to help get you started.

- Turn to pages 30 and 31 to check your answers. (Try all the activities and challenges before you look at the answers.)

- Turn to page 32 for definitions of some words and terms used in this book.

Math Facts and Data

To complete some of the math activities, you will need information from a DATA BOX, which looks like this.

Thermometer Facts
- Many different types of electronic, or digital, thermometers are available today. Some measure body temperature by putting a probe under the arm or in the mouth. With tympanic thermometers, the probe goes into the ear.
- Mercury thermometers are rarely used these days because the mercury inside them is dangerous. If a mercury thermometer accidentally breaks, it is very important to avoid getting the mercury on your skin.

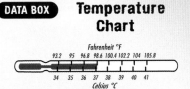

DATA BOX

Temperature Chart

Fahrenheit °F
93.2 95 96.8 98.6 100.4 102.2 104 105.8

34 35 36 37 38 39 40 41
Celsius °C

Temperature is measured using a thermometer. The normal body temperature for humans is 98.6 °F. A nurse may take a patient's temperature many times during a particular period to see whether it is rising or falling. This graph shows the temperature over the course of one day for a patient who arrived in the ER at 8:00 a.m.

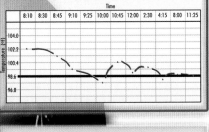

| Time | 8:10 | 8:30 | 8:45 | 9:10 | 9:25 | 10:00 | 10:45 | 12:00 | 2:30 | 4:15 | 8:00 | 11:25 |

Temperature (°F): 104.0 102.2 100.4 98.6 96.8

Math Challenge

Blue boxes, like this one, have extra math questions to challenge you. Give them a try!

Math Challenge

These are the normal body temperatures of seven animals. How much cooler or warmer are their bodies than the normal body temperature of a human?

blue whale	95.9 °F
cow	101.3 °F
dog	100.5 °F
elephant	96.6 °F
ostrich	103.5 °F
owl	104.0 °F
polar bear	98.6 °F

Digital thermometers give an accurate measurement of temperature in less than ten seconds.

Hypothermia Fact
Patients who have hypothermia, which means dangerously low body temperatures, can often be warmed up with warm-air blankets. These blankets are made up of two sheets of thin material stuck together. One of the sheets has a hole in it through which warm air is blown from a special machine. After the blanket fills up with warm air, it is placed on top of the patient.

15

You will find lots of amazing details about emergency rooms and medical care in FACT boxes that look like this.

Doctors and nurses in a hospital emergency room (ER) take care of all kinds of medical problems. They have to know how to treat people who have been injured in accidents as well as people who suddenly become seriously ill, such as having a stroke or a severe asthma attack. Often, people make their own way to a hospital, but in some cases, an ambulance must be called to provide transportation and immediate medical care. Paramedics from the ambulance give first aid treatments before or while taking patients to the closest or the most appropriate hospitals.

Emergency Work

The map in the DATA BOX on page 7 shows routes the ambulance could take to get from the hospital to the scene of an accident.

1) Describe the shortest route, telling the driver whether to turn left or right at each junction.
   a) How many left turns will the driver make?
   b) How many right turns?

2) Find the shortest route that avoids the traffic lights.
   a) How many left turns will the driver make?
   b) How many right turns?

3) On the way back to the hospital, the driver wants to avoid both the traffic lights and the speed bumps.
   a) How many left turns will the driver make?
   b) How many right turns?

Math Challenge

Use the map in the DATA BOX on page 7 to answer this question.

How far is the shortest distance from the scene of the accident to the hospital? Give your answer in miles.

Emergency Driving Facts

• Ambulances use sirens and flashing lights when going to and from emergencies to alert other vehicles, as well as pedestrians, to move out of the way.
• Paramedics spend about three weeks learning how to drive an ambulance. At the end of their training, they have to pass a test to show their advanced driving skills.

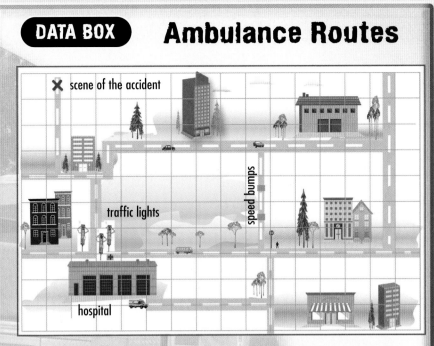

DATA BOX — Ambulance Routes

Each line segment
(—) = 660 feet

The ambulance driver must know the roads well and be clear about the exact location of the accident scene. After giving the accident victim first aid, paramedics must get the injured person to the hospital as quickly as possible.

Paramedics use gurneys, which are cots, or stretchers, that have wheels, to move patients into and out of ambulances.

First Aid Treatments

These are some of the ways paramedics help patients with various injuries.

arm injury – Put the arm in a sling.

leg injury – Put a splint on the leg.

heavily bleeding wound – Apply a gauze dressing and a bandage and elevate the area of the wound to help reduce the bleeding.

pain – Give the patient a special kind of pain-relieving gas to breathe.

unconsciousness – Lay the patient on his or her side with the head tilted slightly upward (the recovery position). This position reduces the patient's risk of choking while unconscious.

back or neck injury – Strap the patient onto a special board and place foam blocks on either side of his or her head to guard against any further injury while the person is being moved.

When a patient arrives at the ER, he or she is usually met by a triage (pronounced "tree-ahj") nurse. This nurse must determine how serious the patient's illness or injury is and decide whether or not the patient's medical needs are urgent. In emergency rooms, patients with the most serious problems are treated first. Those with less serious problems must wait. The triage nurse must also find out the patient's personal details. The hospital needs to know each patient's name, address, date of birth, and medical history.

Emergency Work

The DATA BOX at the top of page 9 shows the personal details for six patients. Look at each patient's date of birth (DOB) and read the clues in the speech bubbles below to figure out the names of these people.

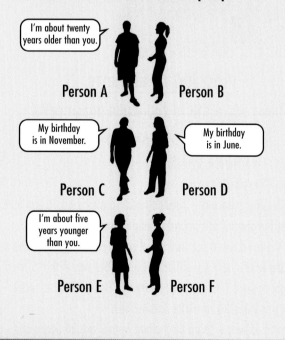

I'm about twenty years older than you.

Person A   Person B

My birthday is in November.   My birthday is in June.

Person C   Person D

I'm about five years younger than you.

Person E   Person F

Patients who have difficulty breathing are put into the red triage category and are treated immediately.

DATA BOX — Patients' Details

Last name: Court
First name: Camelia
DOB: 11-6-1993
Sex: female
Address: 1710 Green Street

Last name: Smith
First name: Susan
DOB: 6-25-1977
Sex: female
Address: 2906 Elm Avenue

Last name: Collins
First name: Jack
DOB: 7-13-1958
Sex: male
Address: 1107 Payton Place

Last name: Barber
First name: Betty
DOB: 9-3-1988
Sex: female
Address: 5820 Mill Road

Last name: Miller
First name: Arthur
DOB: 11-25-1959
Sex: male
Address: 633 Lowry Lane

Last name: Gorasia
First name: Deepa
DOB: 1-8-1978
Sex: female
Address: 3664 Main Street

DATA BOX — Triage Colors

A triage nurse puts emergency room patients into the following color categories, according to the patients' symptoms and the nurse's assessments. Each patient's triage color is printed on his or her chart to tell the doctor how serious that person's condition is and how quickly the patient should be seen.

Red – Immediate: Patient needs to be seen immediately.

Orange – Very Urgent: Patient needs to be seen within ten minutes of arrival.

Yellow – Urgent: Patient needs to be seen within one hour of arrival.

Green – Standard: Patient should be seen within two hours of arrival.

Blue – Not Urgent: Patient should be seen within four hours of arrival.

Math Challenge

Use the information in both of the DATA BOXES on this page, along with the clues below, to figure out the triage color for each of the six patients.

- The youngest patient has trouble breathing and needs to be seen immediately.
- The oldest patient has a sprained ankle and should be seen within two hours of arrival.
- Betty Barber has been put into the "not urgent" category.
- Susan Smith is bleeding and needs to be seen within ten minutes of her arrival.
- Another female patient has burns and needs to be seen within one hour of her arrival.
- The sixth patient has been put into the yellow category.

A hospital's emergency department has several different areas and rooms. Each area has the special equipment doctors need to treat particular medical conditions. A resuscitation room, for example, has the equipment a doctor needs to restart a patient's heart. The pediatric area has medical equipment to treat children and toys for the children to play with. Some ER patients are taken to cubicles, others are asked to stay in a waiting area. Before a patient is seen by a doctor, a nurse assesses the person's condition, which includes doing a set of tests to check vital signs — heart rate, blood pressure, temperature, and breathing.

Emergency Work

The DATA BOX on page 11 shows some of the most common conditions and kinds of injuries that bring people to the ER. Look at the pictograph to see how many people suffered from each condition during one morning in a hospital's emergency department.

Use the information in the pictograph to answer these questions.

1) What is the most common condition?

2) What is the least common condition?

3) How many patients had
    a) chest pains?
    b) wounds?
    c) suspected broken bones?
    d) abdominal pains?

4) How many more patients had breathing difficulties than had chest pains?

5) How many fewer patients had wounds than had suspected broken bones?

6) In total, how many patients were seen in the ER that morning?

A doctor or a nurse uses a stethoscope to listen to a patient's heart and lungs

Emergency Facts

To help determine a patient's condition, a triage nurse will do one or more of the following tests.

- Place an electronic probe on the patient's finger to measure his or her pulse rate and to check the oxygen levels in the blood.
- Check the patient's breathing, or respiratory rate, by counting the number of breaths taken in one minute.
- Take the patient's temperature.
- Ask the patient for a urine specimen or perform a skin prick test to check the patient's blood sugar levels.

DATA BOX

Conditions of ER Patients

This pictograph shows how many patients visited a hospital's ER in one morning, seeking treatment for the medical conditions listed.

Key ☹ = 3 people

wounds	☹☹☹☹☹☹☹☹☹☹
suspected broken bones	☹☹☹☹☹☹☹☹☹☹☹☹◔
unconsciousness or semiconsciousness	☹☹☹
chest pains	☹☹☹☹☹
breathing difficulties	☹☹☹☹☹☹☹☹◔
abdominal pains	☹☹☹☹☹☹☹◑
other conditions	☹☹☹☹☹☹☹☹☹

Math Challenge

If an ER treats 250 patients a day, about how many patients will be treated there in one month?

11

Taking a person's pulse means finding out how quickly his or her heart is beating and whether it is beating regularly, at a normal rhythm. A patient's pulse, or heart rate, might be high for many reasons, ranging from having recently exercised to being in shock or having heart problems. A nurse may also check a patient's heart rate by listening to it through a stethoscope. At the same time the heart rate is being measured, an ER nurse will also measure blood pressure to find out how hard the blood is being pumped through the body. For serious heart conditions, a person might be attached to a heart rate monitor, which is a machine that shows the heart beat on a screen.

Emergency Work

The DATA BOX on page 13 contains a table showing the expected pulse rates for children and adults at different ages. An ER nurse can determine whether a patient has a pulse rate outside the expected range, which might indicate that the patient has a heart problem.

The list below shows the pulse rates for six children of different ages. Using the number of times each child's heart beats in fifteen seconds, figure out each child's pulse rate per minute. Then use the information in the DATA BOX on page 13 to decide which of these children may have a heart problem.

child's name	child's age	number of heart beats in 15 seconds
Jane	4 years	25
Luke	6 months	35
Dillon	7 years	36
Urvi	13 years	29
Molly	1 year	31
Paige	9 years	19

The piece of medical equipment that measures blood pressure is called a sphygmomanometer (pronounced spig-moh-man-AH-meh-tur).

DATA BOX Pulse Rate

A pulse rate is the number of heart beats per minute. A resting pulse rate is how fast the heart beats when a person is not doing any exercise. The table below shows the expected pulse rates for different ages.

age range	expected number of heart beats per minute
less than 12 months old	between 110 and 160
1 to 2 years old	between 100 and 150
3 to 5 years old	between 95 and 140
6 to 12 years old	between 80 and 120
more than 12 years old	between 60 and 100

To measure heart rate, count the number of times the heart beats in 15 seconds (one-quarter of a minute), then multiply this number by 4 to get the number of heart beats per minute.

Math Challenge

The pulse rates of six adults are shown below. How many times would each person's heart beat in 15 seconds (one-quarter of a minute)?

a) 80 beats per minute   d) 72 beats per minute
b) 60 beats per minute   e) 68 beats per minute
c) 52 beats per minute   f) 88 beats per minute

Heart Rate Fact

While they are waiting for test results, some ER patients are put on heart rate monitors. These monitors display the heart rate on a screen so everyone knows immediately if there is a problem. A patient may be put on a monitor if his or her heart rate is very slow (less than 60 beats per minute) or very fast (more than 120 beats per minute), or if the heart beat is irregular. Usually, very sick patients and patients who have chest pains will have their heart rates monitored.

Blood Pressure Fact

To check a patient's blood pressure, a nurse wraps an inflatable cuff around the top of the patient's arm. Then the nurse puts a stethoscope on the patient's forearm, in front of the elbow, and inflates the cuff until it is tight around the upper arm. As the nurse lets the air out of the cuff, the sound of the patient's heart beat can be heard through the stethoscope, and the blood pressure reading can be seen on a pressure gauge.

Another job for an ER nurse is taking a patient's temperature. A body temperature that is too high or too low can be very serious. When body temperature is high, the patient has a fever and feels warm or hot to the touch. Body temperature that is too low can affect the brain, making the person unable to think clearly or move normally. When a patient's temperature is not normal, a doctor or a nurse will take steps to correct it. In the case of a fever, a nurse might use a damp cloth, or even ice packs, to cool the patient. For a low temperature, or hypothermia, the nurse might cover the patient with a warm-air blanket.

Emergency Work

The DATA BOX on page 15 contains a graph that records a patient's body temperature for one day. Use the graph to help you answer these questions.

1) What was the patient's temperature at
   a) 8:10?
   b) 10:45?
   c) 9:10?

2) At what time was the temperature the lowest?

3) At what time was the temperature 101.3 °F?

4) How many minutes after the first time the temperature was taken was it taken again?

First Aid Tips

• When you are stuck in very cold conditions, do not jump around. The exercise will make you lose heat more quickly.
• About 30 percent of body heat is lost from the head, so make sure you head is covered.

Thermometer Facts

- Many different types of electronic, or digital, thermometers are available today. Some measure body temperature by putting a probe under the arm or in the mouth. With tympanic thermometers, the probe goes into the ear.
- Mercury thermometers are rarely used these days because the mercury inside them is dangerous. If a mercury thermometer accidentally breaks, it is very important to avoid getting the mercury on your skin.

DATA BOX

Temperature Chart

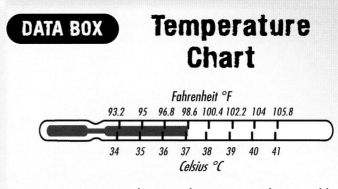

Temperature is measured using a thermometer. The normal body temperature for humans is 98.6 °F. A nurse may take a patient's temperature many times during a particular period to see whether it is rising or falling. This graph shows the temperature over the course of one day for a patient who arrived in the ER at 8:00 a.m.

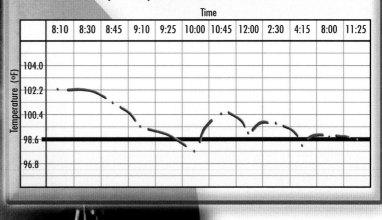

Math Challenge

These are the normal body temperatures of seven animals. How much cooler or warmer are their bodies than the normal body temperature of a human?

blue whale	95.9 °F
cow	101.3 °F
dog	100.5 °F
elephant	96.6 °F
ostrich	103.5 °F
owl	104.0 °F
polar bear	98.6 °F

Digital thermometers give an accurate measurement of temperature in less than ten seconds.

Hypothermia Fact

Patients who have hypothermia, which means dangerously low body temperatures, can often be warmed up with warm-air blankets. These blankets are made up of two sheets of thin material stuck together. One of the sheets has a hole in it through which warm air is blown from a special machine. After the blanket fills up with warm air, it is placed on top of the patient.

BREATHING

Emergency rooms often treat people with breathing difficulties, such as asthma attacks. Asthma is the most common cause of breathing problems in children. It is an illness in which the air passages through which people breathe tighten, causing wheezing, gasping, and shortness of breath. When an asthma patient arrives at the ER, a nurse usually asks the person to blow into a peak flow meter. This piece of equipment measures how much breath the person can blow out in less than a second. Readings from the peak flow meter tell the nurse how serious the patient's condition is and help decide appropriate treatment.

Emergency Work

The DATA BOX at the top of page 17 contains a table of peak flow meter readings for five childen.

What is the difference between the expected and actual readings for

1) Ella? 2) Robbie? 3) Ben? 4) Zack? 5) Jess?

Math Challenge

Use the graph in the DATA BOX at the bottom of page 17 to help you answer these questions.

1) What is the approximate expected peak flow rate for a height of
   a) 58 inches?
   b) 62 inches?
   c) 46 inches?

2) What is the approximate height for an expected peak flow rate of
   a) 500 L/min.?
   b) 420 L/min.?
   c) 210 L/min.?

DATA BOX Peak Flow Meter

The amount of breath a child can blow out is usually related to the child's height. Taller children generally blow out more than shorter children. People who have asthma are not able to blow out as much and show lower readings on a peak flow meter.

Example: Ella is 50 inches tall. Normally, the peak flow reading for a child her height would be 260 liters per minute (L/min.), but because Ella has asthma, she can blow out only 150 L/min.

To get a peak flow reading, a patient has to blow as strong a breath as possible into the tube of a peak flow meter.

Peak Flow Readings

Name	Expected reading (L/min.)	Actual reading (L/min.)
Ella	260	150
Robbie	470	300
Ben	330	190
Zack	210	170
Jess	520	380

DATA BOX Peak Flow at Different Heights

This graph shows the expected peak flow rates for people of different heights.

The red lines show how to find the expected reading for Ella's height of 50 inches.

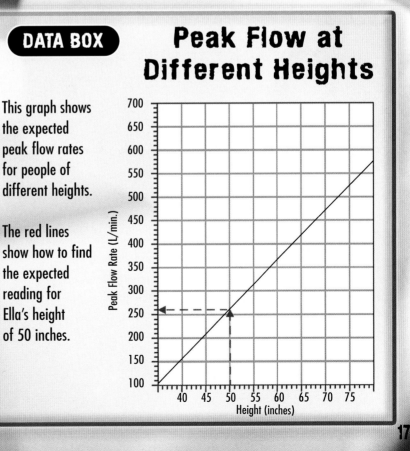

BLOOD WORK AND OTHER TESTS

After the ER's initial assessment of a patient's condition, a specific medical problem still might not be clear, and further testing may be needed. Common testing includes checking blood and urine for diseases and using scanning equipment, such as X-ray, ultrasound, computerized axial tomography (CT or CAT), or Magnetic Resonance Imaging (MRI) machines. The additional tests help doctors pinpoint the causes of problems and decide how best to treat them. Some ER patients are given these tests immediately. Others are sent home and arrange to have the tests done later.

Emergency Work

To keep track of changes in medical conditions, doctors and nurses need to be good at recognizing whether numbers are increasing or decreasing in value and by how much. They also need to be good at predicting what might happen next.

Can you figure out the next three numbers in each of these sequences?

1) 2, 4, 6, 8, 10, 12, . . .
2) 90, 80, 70, 60, 50, 40, . . .
3) 30, 35, 40, 45, 50, 55, 60, . . .
4) 3, 6, 9, 12, 15, 18, . . .
5) 2, 7, 12, 17, 22, 27, 32, 37, . . .
6) $\frac{1}{2}$, 1, 1$\frac{1}{2}$, 2, 2$\frac{1}{2}$, 3, . . .
7) 3, 7, 11, 15, 19, 23, . . .
8) 3, 2, 1, 0, −1, −2, −3, −4, . . .

> *To decide what further tests a patient needs, an ER doctor will often discuss a patient's condition with a doctor who specializes in a certain field of medicine.*

Blood Facts

An adult's blood volume is approximately 7 percent of body weight.
- A 220-pound adult has approximately 15 pints of blood.
- A 155-pound adult has approximately 10½ pints of blood.
- A 110-pound adult has approximately 8 pints of blood.

Compared to adults, children have much less blood.
- A 22-pound child has approximately 1.7 pints of blood.

DATA BOX

Blood Collection Tubes

When blood is taken to be tested, it is put into a blood collection tube. Blood tubes come in different sizes. Each size tube has a different colored stopper.

3 1/2 ml

Tubes with **red stoppers** hold 3 1/2 milliliters (ml) of blood. These tubes are used to test patients for anemia, or having too few red blood cells.

7 1/2 ml

Tubes with **brown stoppers** hold 7 1/2 ml. They are used to check a patient's body salts.

2 1/2 ml

Tubes with **yellow stoppers** hold 2 1/2 ml and are used to check blood sugar levels.

4 1/2 ml

Tubes with **blue stoppers** hold 4 1/2 ml of blood. They are used to find out a patient's blood type. There are four blood groups, A, B, AB, and O. Most people are either blood group O or A.

Math Challenge

A nurse uses two of the blood collection tubes shown in the DATA BOX above and fills both of them with blood.

What color stoppers do the two bottles have if, together, they hold a total of

1) 6 ml?

2) 7 ml?

3) 8 ml?

4) 10 ml?

When the type and extent of a patient's injuries or illness is finally determined, a doctor will decide what kind of medical treatment is necessary. Treatments can include putting a broken limb in a plaster cast, prescribing a particular medication or drug, giving an injection, or even ordering an operation. The doctor will explain to the patient what will be happening and why. When deciding how much of a drug to use, a doctor often needs to think about how old the patient is or how much the patient weighs. Whether given a drug by mouth or injection, a child usually needs much less of it than an adult.

Emergency Work

Use the information in the DATA BOX on page 21 to help you figure out how much of each kind of medicine to give a child in an injection.

1) How much antibiotic should be given to a child who weighs
   a) 34 pounds?   b) 48 pounds?   c) 32 pounds?

2) How much painkiller should be given to a child who weighs
   a) 30 pounds?   b) 26 pounds?   c) 38 pounds?

3) How much steroid should be given to a child who weighs
   a) 50 pounds?   b) 60 pounds?

4) How much antihistamine should be given to a child who weighs
   a) 40 pounds?   b) 70 pounds?

Medicine Facts

• Medicine taken by mouth, or orally, can be a tablet, a capsule, or a liquid. Tablets and capsules are fixed doses of medicine. Children are normally given liquid medicine because smaller doses can be measured, and liquid medicine is easier to swallow than tablets or capsules.
• Patients who suffer with breathing difficulties such as asthma usually take their medicine through a device called an inhaler. Medicine from an inhaler is either a mist or a dry powder that is breathed in through the mouth and goes straight into the lungs.

DATA BOX

How Much Medicine to Give a Child by Injection

Because children are smaller than adults, the doses of medicines or drugs they need are usually smaller than doses for adults. The list below explains how to calculate, in milligrams (mg), the amounts of four different kinds of medicines to give a child by injection.

antibiotics For every pound of body weight, give 100 mg of antibiotic injection. If the child weighs more than 40 pounds, give only 4,000 mg of antibiotic.

painkillers Divide the child's weight by 10, then multiply by 200. The answer tells you how many mg of painkiller injection to give.

steroids Multiply the child's weight by 4, then divide by 100. The answer tells you how many mg of steroid injection to give.

antihistamines For every pound of body weight, give 10 mg of antihistamine injection, up to 500 mg.

Before giving an injection, a doctor or nurse always uses antiseptic to clean the patient's skin around the place where the needle will be inserted.

Math Challenge

Some of these cards show fractions and others show division. Match pairs of cards that will give the same answers

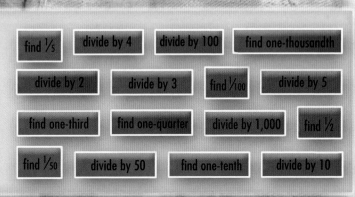

find ⅕	divide by 4	divide by 100	find one-thousandth
divide by 2	divide by 3	find ⅟₁₀₀	divide by 5
find one-third	find one-quarter	divide by 1,000	find ½
find ⅟₅₀	divide by 50	find one-tenth	divide by 10

BROKEN BONES

ome of the most common injuries treated in the ER are sprains and broken bones. To find out if a patient has a broken bone, an ER doctor will have an X-ray taken. The person who takes the X-ray is called a radiographer or an X-ray technologist. The patient is taken to a special room, where an X-ray machine is positioned over the injured part of the body. The radiographer has to estimate the dose of radiation and the exposure time needed to get a good picture. This information is entered into a computer, and, with a press of a button, the X-ray is taken. X-ray film is processed in a machine similar to the machines that develop regular photographs. Then the film is ready for a doctor to look at.

Emergency Work

A sling is used to protect a sprain or a broken bone from too much movement and further injury. It is normally made using a triangular piece of material.

1) Identify each sling above as a scalene, isosceles, or equilateral triangle.

2) Which of these triangles have right angles?

Treatment Facts

Bones are held together by ligaments. A sprain occurs when a ligament has been stretched. When a person sprains his or her ankle, the ankle needs to be rested and kept elevated, or in a raised postion. Ice can help reduce the swelling of the sprain and, often, a support bandage is wrapped around the ankle. Support bandages are tubes or rolls of elastic material. A sprained wrist also needs to be rested and may be placed in an sling to help avoid a lot of movement.

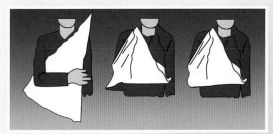

You can make a sling out of a
square scarf folded in half diagonally.

DATA BOX

X-Ray Doses

Body Part	Dose
arm	4
leg	5
knee	3
elbow	3
ankle	2
wrist	1
hip	40
chest	2
skull	50
abdomen	70

An X-ray machine uses radiation to take pictures of the human body. Different doses of radiation are needed for X-rays of different body parts. The dose depends on the size of the patient and the body part being x-rayed. The table to the left shows the radiation doses for each part of a child's body.

Note: Too much radiation can be dangerous. People who operate X-ray machines must wear special badges to show how much radiation they are exposed to while they are working.

Doctors who look at, or read, X-rays are called radiologists.

Math Challenge

Use the table in the DATA BOX above to help you answer these questions.

1) How much larger is
   a) the leg dose than the wrist dose?
   b) the skull dose than the elbow dose?
   c) the hip dose than the wrist dose?

2) The hip dose is 10 times larger than the arm dose. How many times larger is
   a) the skull dose than the leg dose?
   b) the hip dose than the ankle dose?
   c) the abdomen dose than the chest dose?

DRUG CHART

While a patient is still in the ER, the doctor needs to write a summary that records the treatments given to the patient and suggests appropriate follow-up care. Some patients need to stay in the hospital, but many are discharged and are allowed to go home. Often, a patient's follow-up care includes taking drugs. Before a doctor prescribes any drugs, however, he or she must check that the patient is not already taking medicines that may react with the new drug. The doctor must also be sure that the patient does not have any drug allergies. Doctors record prescribed medicines for patients on drug charts.

A patient's records help doctors decide how much medicine to give.

Emergency Work

The DATA BOX on page 25 has a table showing the drugs prescribed for four patients, including how many tablets to take and how often and how long to take them. Use the information in the table to answer these questions.

1) How many tablets, in total, will be taken by
   a) Ivan Peterson?
   b) Justine Bedlow?
   c) Frank Fitch?
   d) Simon Brant?

2) If the doctor says that each patient should take two tablets at a time, at regular intervals throughout a 24-hour day, how many hours apart would the tablets be taken by
   a) Ivan Peterson?
   b) Justine Bedlow?
   c) Frank Fitch?
   d) Simon Brant?

Most medicine for adults is given in the form of tablets.

Drug Cycles

Name of Patient	Prescribed Drug	Number of Tablets (per day)	Number of Days
Ivan Peterson	steroid tablets	8	3
Justine Bedlow	antihistamines	6	2
Frank Fitch	antibiotics	4	5
Simon Brant	painkillers	8	7

Some drugs are to be taken at regular time intervals throughout the day. Others, such as painkillers, are to be taken only when the patient needs them. A doctor may give specific instructions such as "Take one or two tablets every six hours, as needed."

Math Challenge

1) A patient is told to take 1 tablet every 8 hours for 1 day.
   a) If the first tablet is taken at 8:00 a.m., at what times are the other tablets taken?
   b) If the first tablet is taken at 6:30 a.m., at what times are the other tablets taken?

2) A patient is told to take 1 tablet every 6 hours for 1 day.
   a) If the first tablet is taken at 7:00 p.m., at what times are the other tablets taken?
   b) If the first tablet is taken at 4:30 a.m., at what times are the other tablets taken?

Medicine Facts

Many medicines have two names. The "generic" name is the main ingredient of the tablet or injection. The "trade" name is the name given to the medicine by the company that makes it. Paracetamol is the generic name for a type of painkiller. Trade names for paracetamol include Panadol and Tylenol.

The role of the ER is to provide medical care for people with urgent needs. After an emergency has been taken care of, the patient is moved out of the ER. If the injury or illness is not too serious, the patient is discharged from the hospital and is sent home. Some patients, however, are moved to other areas, or wards, in the hospital for further treatment. Patients treated in the ER for head injuries or very high fevers, for example, are usually admitted to the hospital, for at least a few days, for continued observation. The ER doctor might recommend that a patient be looked at frequently and have vital signs checked regularly.

Emergency Work

The DATA BOX on page 27 contains an ER doctor's summary and a plan telling how often the patient should be checked while in the hospital.

How many times will the patient be checked during the first eight hours?

Follow-up Facts

• Some patients are discharged with a prescription from an ER doctor for medicine or drugs. The prescription must be taken to a pharmacy, where a pharmacist counts out the correct number of tablets and writes instructions on the container that explain how to take the medicine.

• Some discharged patients are asked to come back to the hospital, later on, for a checkup. They can make appointments to see hospital doctors as outpatients.

• An ER doctor may write a letter to a patient's family doctor, or general practitioner (GP), so the GP will know about any ER tests or treatments and whether he or she needs to see the patient for a checkup.

DATA BOX

Patient's Summary

The patient's summary below describes follow-up care for a child who was injured while playing at school.

○○○○○○○○○○○○○○○

Complaint: head injury

Background: fell off monkey bars on playground and bumped head

Examination: bruise on right side of forehead, otherwise normal

Diagnosis: minor head injury

Plan: observations every fifteen minutes for the first hour, every thirty minutes for the next two hours, and once each hour for the next five hours.

Property of Dexter
Middle School Library

A doctor must check a patient's medical records carefully before allowing the patient to go home.

Math Challenge

Approximately one in every five patients seen in the ER is admitted to the hospital. The rest are discharged, or sent home.

What percentage of patients is sent home?

MATH TIPS

PAGES 6-7

Math Challenge

Remember that 1 mile = 5,280 feet, so 660 feet = $\frac{1}{8}$ mile (5,280 ÷ 8 = 660).

PAGES 8-9

Emergency Work

When writing dates, the months can be numbered from 1 through 12. January is the first month (1) and December is the twelfth month (12). Dates written as numbers show the month, day, and year.

Example: 2-4-1991 is the second month (February), the fourth day, in the year 1991, or February 4, 1991.

PAGES 10-11

Math Challenge

One month is about 30 days, so you can multiply 250 by 3, then multiply that answer by 10 to find the number of patients treated in one month.

PAGES 12-13

Emergency Work

To multiply by 4, double the number, then double the new number.

Example: 25 x 4   Double 25 (25 x 2) = 50
                        Double 50 (50 x 2) = 100
                        So 25 x 4 = 100

Math Challenge

To divide by 4, halve the number, then halve the new number.

Example: 180 ÷ 4   Half of 180 (180 ÷ 2) = 90
                        Half of 90 (90 ÷ 2) = 45
                        So 180 ÷ 4 = 45

PAGES 14-15

TOP TIP: Temperature is the measure of how hot or cold something is. The unit of measurement for temperature is degrees Fahrenheit or degrees Celsius, which are written using the symbols °F or °C.

PAGES 16-17

Math Challenge

When reading the graph to find the peak flow rate for a given height, read straight up from the height until you reach the diagonal line, then read across to the peak flow rate.

When reading the graph to find the height for a given peak flow rate, read straight across from the peak flow rate until you reach the diagonal line, then read down to the height.

PAGES 18-19

Emergency Work

If you are not sure how a number sequence continues, find the difference between the numbers, as shown in the example below.

Example:

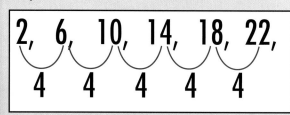

The difference between each number in this sequence is 4, so the next number will be 4 more than 22, and so on.

PAGES 20–21

Emergency Work

To divide a number by 10, move each of the number's digits one place to the right.

Tth	Th	H	T	U	.	t
		3	4	0		
			3	4	.	0

To divide a number, by 100, move each of the number's digits two places to the right.

Tth	Th	H	T	U	.	t
		3	4	0		
			3	4	.	0
				3	.	4

To divide a number by 50, first divide the number by 100, then double the answer.

PAGES 22–23

Math Challenge

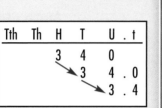

Scalene triangles have no equal sides and no equal angles.

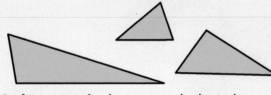

Isosceles triangles have two equal sides and two equal angles.

Equilateral triangles have all equal sides and all equal angles. The angles are all 60°.

PAGES 24–25

Math Challenge

Remember that a.m. means in the morning, between midnight and midday, and p.m. means in the afternoon or evening, between midday and midnight.

PAGES 26–27

Math Challenge

Percent (%) is a special form of a fraction. It means "part of 100." So 50 percent (50%) means $\frac{50}{100}$ or, in its simplest form, $\frac{1}{2}$.

To find the percentage of people admitted to the hospital, figure out what $\frac{1}{5}$ is as a percentage, then subtract that percentage from 100 to find the percentage of people sent home.

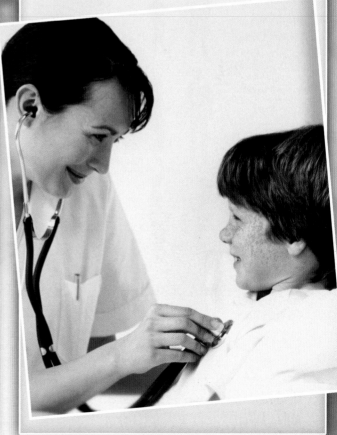

ANSWERS

PAGES 6–7

Emergency Work

After leaving the hospital, the shortest route is to take the first turn **left**, then turn **left** again. At the traffic lights, turn **right**, then **left**, then **right** again.

1) a) 3   b) 2
2) a) 4   b) 3
3) a) 3   b) 4

Math Challenge

2.75 miles

PAGES 8–9

Emergency Work

I'm about 20 years older than you.

Person A
Jack Collins

Person B
Deepa Gorasia

My birthday is in November.

My birthday is in June.

Person C
Arthur Miller

Person D
Susan Smith

I'm about 5 years younger than you.

Person E
Camelia Court

Person F
Betty Barber

Math Challenge

Camelia Court	Red
Jack Collins	Green
Betty Barber	Blue
Susan Smith	Orange
Deepa Gorasia	Yellow
Arthur Miller	Yellow

PAGES 10–11

Emergency Work

1) suspected broken bones
2) unconsciousness or semiconsciousness
3) a) 15   b) 27   c) 31   d) 19
4) 8   5) 4   6) 148

Math Challenge

about 7500 patients

PAGES 12–13

Emergency Work

Jane	100	No problem
Luke	140	No problem
Dillon	144	Pulse is too fast
Urvi	116	Pulse is too fast
Molly	124	No problem
Paige	76	Pulse is too slow

Math Challenge

a) 20   d) 18
b) 15   e) 17
c) 13   f) 22

PAGES 14–15

Emergency Work

1) a) 102.2 °F   b) 100.4 °F   c) 99.5 °F
2) 10:00
3) 08:45
4) 35 minutes

Math Challenge

blue whale	2.7 °F cooler
cow	2.7 °F warmer
dog	1.9 °F warmer
elephant	2.0 °F cooler
ostrich	4.9 °F warmer
owl	5.4 °F warmer
polar bear	same

PAGES 16–17

Emergency Work

1) 110 L/min. 3) 140 L/min. 5) 140 L/min.
2) 170 L/min. 4) 40 L/min.

Math Challenge

1) a) about 350 L/min.   2) a) about 73 inches
   b) about 390 L/min.   b) about 65 inches
   c) about 220 L/min.   c) about 45 inches

PAGES 18–19

Emergency Work

1) 14, 16, 18   5) 42, 47, 52
2) 30, 20, 10   6) 3½, 4, 4½
3) 65, 70, 75   7) 27, 31, 35
4) 21, 24, 27   8) −5, −6, −7

Math Challenge

1) red and yellow   3) red and blue
2) yellow and blue   4) brown and yellow

PAGES 20–21

Emergency Work

1) a) 3,400 mg   b) 4,000 mg   c) 3,200 mg
2) a) 600 mg   b) 520 mg   c) 760 mg
3) a) 2 mg   b) 2.4 mg
4) a) 400 mg   b) 500 mg
   (continued at top of next column)

PAGES 22–23

Emergency Work

1) a) isosceles   b) equilateral   c) scalene
   d) isosceles   e) equilateral   f) scalene
2) triangles c and d each have a right angle

Math Challenge

1) a) 4   b) 47   c) 39
2) a) 10 times   b) 20 times   c) 35 times

PAGES 20–21 (continued)

find one-quarter → divide by 4
find one-tenth → divide by 10
find ⅕ → divide by 5
find ¹⁄₁₀₀ → divide by 100
find ¹⁄₅₀ → divide by 50
find one-thousandth → divide by 1,000
find one-third → divide by 3
find ½ → divide by 2

PAGES 24–25

Emergency Work

1) a) 24   b) 12   c) 20   d) 56
2) a) 6 hours apart   c) 12 hours apart
   b) 8 hours apart   d) 6 hours apart

Math Challenge

1) a) 4:00 p.m. and midnight
   b) 2:30 p.m. and 10:30 p.m.
2) a) 1:00 a.m., 7:00 a.m., and 1:00 p.m.
   b) 10:30 a.m., 4:30 p.m., and 10:30 p.m.

PAGES 26–27

Emergency Work

13 times (4 times in the first hour, twice in the second and third hours, and once in each of the next five hours.)

Math Challenge

80 percent

GLOSSARY

ANTIBIOTIC a strong medicine that kills illness-causing bacteria, or germs

ANTISEPTIC a germ-killing substance for use on the skin and other surfaces

ASSESSMENTS appraisals or determinations of importance or value

ASTHMA an illness in which a person's air passages tighten, causing breathing difficulties

CAPSULE a small, oblong container, usually made of gelatin, that holds a dose of a medicine or drug

GAUZE thin, loosely woven cotton fabric used to dress, or cover, wounds

GENERIC general; describing an entire group or class

HYPOTHERMIA a life-threatening condition in which a person's body temperature drops far below normal

INHALER a handheld device that delivers medicine in the form of a mist or dry powder to help a person breathe

INJECTION forcing medicine or drugs into the body through a needle that pierces the flesh

JUNCTION a place or intersection where two roads meet

LIGAMENTS strong bands of tissue that connect bones or hold body organs in place

LINE SEGMENT the part of a line on which all points lie between two distinct end points

OBSERVATION the process of watching or checking on someone or something on a regular basis

PARAMEDICS people who are trained to give emergency medical care before or while transporting a sick or injured person to a hospital

PEAK FLOW METER a type of medical equipment that measures a person's breathing ability

PEDIATRIC describing the branch of medicine that deals with the health care of infants and children

PICTOGRAPH a graph or diagram that uses pictures to show information

PRESCRIBES writes an order that authorizes a patient's use of drugs

PULSE RATE the rate at which the heart pushes blood around the body

RADIATION energy sent out in the form of radioactive rays or waves

RADIOGRAPHER a person who takes X-rays

REGULAR INTERVALS evenly spaced periods of time within a defined time frame

RESPIRATORY relating to breathing

RESUSCITATION the process of bringing back to life or consciousness

SPLINT stiff or rigid material used to limit the movement of an injured joint or a broken bone

STEROID a type of medicine that can quickly relieve swelling and inflammation

STROKE a sudden loss of physical or mental abilities, caused by a blood clot in the brain

TRIAGE the process of sorting sick or injured people into groups according to their relative needs for medical attention

URGENT requiring immediate attention

Measurement Conversions

1 pint = 0.4732 liters (l)

1 pound = 0.4536 kilograms (kg)

1 mile = 1.609 kilometers (km)

degrees Fahrenheit (°F) − 32 ÷ 1.8 = degrees Celsius (°C)